SPONSORSHIP PAGE

THIS BOOK IS SPONSORED BY

....

....

AS A GIFT TO

....

....

ON THIS DAY

....

'Each one must give as he has decided in his heart,
not reluctantly or under compulsion,
for God loves a cheerful giver.'
(2 Corinthians 9:7, ESV)

BY PRAYER M. MADUEKE

PRAYERS TO PRESERVE YOUR MARRIAGE

BOOK 14 OF 40 PRAYER GIANTS

© 2022 Prayer M. Madueke

ISBN: 979-8488735460

2nd Edition

FREE EBOOKS

In order to say a 'Thank You' for purchasing *Prayers to Preserve your Marriage*, I offer these books to you in appreciation.

> <u>Click here or go to madueke.com/free-gift to download the eBooks now</u> <

MESSAGE FROM THE AUTHOR

PRAYER M. MADUEKE
CHRISTIAN AUTHOR

My name is Prayer Madueke, a spiritual warrior in the Lord's vineyard, an accomplished author, speaker, and expert on spiritual warfare and deliverance. I have published well over 100 books on every area of successful Christian living. I am an acclaimed family and relationship counselor with several titles dealing with critical areas in the lives of the children of God. I travel to several countries each year speaking and conducting deliverance sessions, breaking the yokes of demonic oppression and setting captives free.

It would be a delight to collaborate with you or your ministry in organized crusades, ceremonies, marriages and marriage seminars, special events, church ministration and fellowship for the advancement of God's kingdom here on earth.

You can find all my books on my website: madueke.com.

They have produced many testimonies and I want your testimony to be one too. God bless you.

CHRISTIAN COUNSELLING

We were created for a greater purpose than only survival and God wants us to live a full life.

If you need prayer or counselling, or if you have any other inquiries, please visit the counselling page on my website madueke.com/counselling to know when I will be available for a phone call.

EMAIL NEWSLETTER & ANNOUNCEMENTS

Never miss a message from me again! People who read my newsletters say that they have been one of the most important tools in their Christian walk. The best part is that a subscription is, and always will be, completely free. As a subscriber on my mailing list, you'll be the first to hear about my new book releases, be invited to my weekly prayer sessions, and get reminders about my blog posts and other helpful information.

To subscribe, please visit the newsletter page on my website madueke.com/newsletter.

DEDICATION

This book is dedicated to those who are trusting God to protect and preserve their families. The Lord who sees your sincere dedication will answer your prayers Amen.

TABLE OF CONTENTS

ONE

MARRIAGE IS A LIFE CONTRACT

The Christian vow in a marriage ceremony defines marriage as a lifetime union. The Scripture upholds the same definition:

> Wives, submit yourselves unto your own husbands, as unto the Lord. For the husband is the head of the wife, even as Christ is the head of the church: and he is the savior of the body. Therefore as the church is subject unto Christ, so let the wives be to their own husbands in everything
>
> — EPHESIANS 5:22-24

Wives are commanded to submit to their husbands as unto the Lord. It is a lifetime commitment as long as they both live. Every woman needs prayers to do it so that she will receive blessings in her marriage. The body that does not cooperate with the head would be in trouble. The neck that troubles the head and refuses to carry the head will live without the head. The head will save the body in times of trouble.

Wives that rebel against God's Word do not have peace in their marriages. Separation and divorce do not help matters because the scriptures say that it is not good for man to be alone.

> Husbands, love your wives, even as Christ also loved the church, and gave himself for it; That he might sanctify and cleanse it with the washing of water by the word, That he might present it to himself a glorious church, not having spot, or wrinkle, or any such thing; but that it should be holy and without blemish. So ought men to love their wives as their own bodies. He that loveth his wife loveth himself. For no man ever yet hated his own flesh; but nourisheth and cherisheth it, even as the Lord the church: For we are members of his body, of his flesh, and of his bones. For this cause shall a man leave his father and mother, and shall be

> joined unto his wife, and they two shall be one flesh. This is a great mystery: but I speak concerning Christ and the church. Nevertheless let every one of you in particular so love his wife even as himself; and the wife see that she reverence her husband
>
> — EPHESIANS 5:25-33

If it were good to be alone, God would have allowed man to be without a wife from the beginning. Rather, God said it is not good. Therefore, God's Word is still the same today and forever. There are husbands who find it difficult to love their wives. As a result, they think the only solution is to find a lover outside the home. However, husbands are commanded to love their wives as their own bodies. It must be as Christ loves the church and offered Himself for her.

Failing to love your wife is the same thing as hating your own body. God cannot tell lies. You may not really realize that you hate yourself or your own body by not loving your wife, but it is true because God's Word has said so. More so, many people have realized that it is true. Remember that you promised God that you would love your wife before the officiating minister and the entire crowd during your wedding. In most Christian weddings, the second question to a man by officiating minister is a lifetime commitment. The first question normally goes like this.

(Brother's name) Do you take (sister's name) whose right hand you now hold to be your lawful wedded wife and solemnly promise, God helping you, that you will be a true and devoted husband to her; that you will love her even as Christ love the church, and honor, cherish, protect and care for her for the rest of your lives and that you will keep yourself to her and to her alone until God, by death, shall separate you? If you answered I DO, then you have entered into a lifetime covenant.

The words that were used on your wedding day may not be exactly the same with the above, but the implications are the same. The vow bounds you for life as long as both of you live.

> And he answered and said unto them, Have ye not read, that he which made them at the beginning made them male and female, And said, For this cause shall a man leave father and mother, and shall cleave to his wife: and they twain shall be one flesh? Wherefore they are no more twain, but one flesh. What therefore God hath joined together, let not man put asunder
>
> — MATTHEW 19:4-6

> But from the beginning of the creation God
> made them male and female. For this cause
> shall a man leave his father and mother, and
> cleave to his wife; And they twain shall be one
> flesh: so then they are no more twain, but one
> flesh. What therefore God hath joined together,
> let not man put asunder

— MARK 10:6-9

After you responded, 'I DO,' the minister will ask you to turn to her and make this profession of your faith:

I, (brother's name) according to the Word of God, leave my father and my mother and join myself to you, to be a husband to you. From this moment forward, we shall be one.

The minister then turns to the bride and asks:

(Sister's name) do you take (Brother's name) whose right hand you now hold to be your lawfully wedded husband and solemnly promise, God helping you, that you will be a true and devoted wife to him; that you will submit yourself to him as unto the Lord showing reverence to him as the head of this union, that you will love, honor, cherish and that you will keep yourself to him and to him alone until God, by death, shall separate you? If your response is, I DO, you have made an irrevocable vow for your lifetime.

Meanwhile, for centuries, men have sought for ways to satisfy their desires of putting away their wives. It was not surprising the Pharisees put this question on Jesus:

> The Pharisees also came unto him, tempting him, and saying unto him, Is it lawful for a man to put away his wife for every cause? And he answered and said unto them, Have ye not read, that he which made them at the beginning made them male and female, And said, For this cause shall a man leave father and mother, and shall cleave to his wife: and they twain shall be one flesh? Wherefore they are no more twain, but one flesh. What therefore God hath joined together, let not man put asunder
>
> — MATTHEW 19:3-6

The minister will address the witnesses as follows: Jesus said in the 18th chapter of Matthew's gospel, "*Again, I say unto you that whatever two of you shall agree on earth as touching anything that they shall ask, it shall be done for them of my Father which is in heaven*". You are not here just because of tradition. You are here for a serious purpose to bear witness forever of the "mystery" of the union that takes place this day, and to add your agreement before God to that which takes place.

SOLEMN PRONOUNCEMENT

(To the groom and bride) Join your hands please. A miracle took place when you made Jesus Christ, your Lord and Savior. The power of God that raised Jesus from the dead joined you to Jesus. I want you to understand that this day you are joined together and have become one. The same power that joined you with Jesus when you made Him your Lord and Savior has this day joined you together. Do not ever tamper with this union. Do not ever tamper with this miracle. You are one never to be separated or divorced. As a representative of Jesus Christ before Almighty God and in the name of the father, in the name of the son Jesus and by the power of the Holy Spirit of God, I now pronounce you as one together. You are now husband and wife.

From today, when you agree on things, they will come to pass. You have an awesome power at your disposal. You are going to notice from now a new realm beginning in your life because of a spiritual law that says one can put a thousand to flight and two ten thousand to flight. From now on, your everyday life will be ten times more powerful spiritually than ever before.

Remember; do not ever tamper with the agreement of today. From this day forward, whatever may happen, you are in agreement with this union. Do not ever attempt in any way to cause it to be anything other than a happy union.

TO THE CONGREGATION

In as much as (brother's name) and (sister's name) have both signified that they believed with all their hearts that it is the perfect will of God for them to be joined together in the holy bond of matrimony, have borne witness of this before God and this company and have pledged their fidelity and love each to the other, I, by virtue of the authority vested in me as a minister of the Gospel of Jesus Christ and by the laws of our country now pronounce them as husband and wife, in the name of the Father, and of the Son, and of the Holy Ghost. "What therefore God hath joined together, let no man put asunder".

SIGNING OF MARRIAGE REGISTERS

All the members of the congregation remain quiet in an attitude of worship as marriage register is signed.

BLESSING OF THE UNION

Christ hath redeemed us from the curse of the law, being made a curse for us: for it is written, Cursed is every one that hangeth on a tree: That the blessing of Abraham might come on the Gentiles through Jesus Christ; that we might receive the promise of the Spirit through faith.

— GALATIANS 3:13-14

And all these blessings shall come on thee, and overtake thee, if thou shalt hearken unto the voice of the LORD thy God. Blessed shalt thou be in the city, and blessed shalt thou be in the field. Blessed shall be the fruit of thy body, and the fruit of thy ground, and the fruit of thy cattle, the increase of thy kine, and the flocks of thy sheep. Blessed shall be thy basket and thy store. Blessed shalt thou be when thou comest in, and blessed shalt thou be when thou goest out. The LORD shall cause thine enemies that rise up against thee to be smitten before thy face: they shall come out against thee one way, and flee before thee seven ways. The LORD shall command the blessing upon thee in thy storehouses, and in all that thou settest thine hand unto; and he shall bless thee in the land which the LORD thy God giveth thee. The LORD shall establish thee a holy people unto himself, as he hath sworn unto thee, if thou shalt keep the commandments of the LORD thy God, and walk in his ways. And all people of the earth shall see that thou art called by the name of the LORD; and they shall be afraid of thee. And the LORD shall make thee plenteous in goods, in the fruit of thy body, and in the fruit of thy cattle, and in the fruit of thy ground, in the land which the LORD sware unto thy fathers to give thee. The LORD shall open unto thee his good treasure, the heaven to give the rain unto thy land in his season, and to bless all the work of thine hand: and thou shalt lend unto many nations, and thou shalt not borrow. And the LORD shall make thee the head, and not the tail; and thou shalt be above only, and thou shalt not be beneath; if that thou hearken unto the commandments of the LORD thy God, which I command thee this day, to observe and to do them

— DEUTERONOMY 28:2-13

PRESENTATION TO THE CONGREGATION

Ladies and gentlemen, I present to you, brother and sister (their names

This is what is called marriage, vow or covenant. Yours might not be the exact words, but they all lead to the same end, whether it is done in a church, court or according to tradition. Marriage is for life and a lifetime contract.

TWO

WHAT IS A COVENANT?

Most people do not know that a vow or covenant is a very serious thing. It is even more serious when it is a marriage vow. A marriage vow is more binding than ordinary vows. A covenant is a mutual understanding between two or more parties, each binding himself to fulfill specific obligations. It is a legal agreement to do or not to do certain things.

Marriage covenant empowers people to live in families, rear children and live in local community or nation. The Word of God captured this essence:

God setteth the solitary in families: he bringeth

out those which are bound with chains: but the

rebellious dwell in a dry land

— PSALMS 68:6

Lo, children are a heritage of the LORD: and the fruit of the womb is his reward

— PSALMS 127:3

⁵And Moses commanded the children of Israel according to the word of the LORD, saying, The tribe of the sons of Joseph hath said well. ⁶This is the thing which the LORD doth command concerning the daughters of Zelophehad, saying, Let them marry to whom they think best; only to the family of the tribe of their father shall they marry. ⁷So shall not the inheritance of the children of Israel remove from tribe to tribe: for every one of the children of Israel shall keep himself to the inheritance of the tribe of his fathers. ⁸And every daughter, that possesseth an inheritance in any tribe of the children of Israel, shall be wife unto one of the family of the tribe of her father, that the children of Israel may enjoy every man the inheritance of his fathers. ⁹Neither shall the inheritance remove from one tribe to another tribe; but every one of the tribes of the children

of Israel shall keep himself to his own

inheritance. ¹³These are the commandments and

the judgments, which the LORD commanded by

the hand of Moses unto the children of Israel in

the plains of Moab by Jordan near Jericho

— NUMBERS 36:5-9, 13

Marriage is also designed for preservation of purity and holiness in the church and community.

²Nevertheless, to avoid fornication, let every

man have his own wife, and let every woman

have her own husband. ⁹But if they cannot

contain, let them marry: for it is better to marry

than to burn. ¹⁰And unto the married I

command, yet not I, but the Lord, Let not the

wife depart from her husband: ¹¹But and if she

depart, let her remain unmarried, or be

reconciled to her husband: and let not the

husband put away his wife

— 1 CORINTHIANS 7:2, 9-11

Marriage is one of God's methods to keep men and women free from immorality. God did not make any provision in His Word for people to have sexual relationships except through marriage. Any open or secret love among people can bring curse, but marriage brings completeness and fulfillment of true living in life.

And it shall come to pass, if they will not believe also these two signs, neither hearken unto thy voice, that thou shalt take of the water of the river, and pour it upon the dry land: and the water which thou takest out of the river shall become blood upon the dry land. And Moses said unto the LORD, O my Lord, I am not eloquent, neither heretofore, nor since thou hast spoken unto thy servant: but I am slow of speech, and of a slow tongue. And the LORD said unto him, Who hath made man's mouth? Or who maketh the dumb, or deaf, or the seeing, or the blind? Have not I the LORD?

— EXODUS 4:9–11

Marriage provides true fellowship, comfort, companionship and fellowship. Our likenesses and differences complement one another in a marriage relationship.

> And God blessed Noah and his sons, and said unto them, Be fruitful, and multiply, and replenish the earth
>
> — GENESIS 9:1

Marriage also is to complement God's work of procreation. Generally, covenant is designed to establish friendship, procure assistance in wars and guarantee mutual protection.

> Then Jonathan and David made a covenant, because he loved him as his own soul
>
> — 1 SAMUEL 18:3

> And the LORD sent thee on a journey, and said, Go and utterly destroy the sinners the Amalekites, and fight against them until they be consumed. Wherefore then didst thou not obey the voice of the LORD, but didst fly upon the spoil, and didst evil in the sight of the LORD?

— 1 SAMUEL 15:18-19

And they said, We saw certainly that the LORD
was with thee: and we said, Let there be now an
oath betwixt us, even betwixt us and thee, and
let us make a covenant with thee; That thou wilt
do us no hurt, as we have not touched thee, and
as we have done unto thee nothing but good,
and have sent thee away in peace: thou art now
the blessed of the LORD

— GENESIS 26:28-29

As soon as marriage vows are completed and confirmed, it
cannot be altered.

Brethren, I speak after the manner of men;
Though it be but a man's covenant, yet if it be
confirmed, no man disannulleth, or addeth
thereto

— GALATIANS 3:15

Marriage is an irrevocable commitment. It comes into effect by
answering marriage vows. Holding of hands and signing the

marriage register. It is sealed with a kiss, a hug and sexual relationship. Marriage covenant is the most powerful covenant on earth and cannot be toyed with.

> Yet ye say, Wherefore? Because the LORD hath been witness between thee and the wife of thy youth, against whom thou hast dealt treacherously: yet is she thy companion, and the wife of thy covenant. And did not he make one? Yet had he the residue of the spirit. And wherefore one? That he might seek a godly seed. Therefore take heed to your spirit, and let none deal treacherously against the wife of his youth
>
> — MALACHI 2:14-15

THREE

DEALING WITH FAMILY PROBLEMS

Devil has deployed abundant marital challenges to shake families of the earth. While majority of people attempt to solve their family problems by running away from them, few that are wise run to God to deliver them from troubles. Others ironically opt for easy way outs which devil provides to them. This option would eventually put them into greater bondage. Learn how to endure because the bible put it this way:

> Man that is born of a woman is of few days, and full of trouble
>
> — JOB 14:1

Jesus saith unto him, I am the way, the truth,
and the life: no man cometh unto the Father,
but by me

— JOHN 14:6

The scripture revealed that troubles must come, and the only way out is through Lord Jesus, who has provided the right way. Any other way leads to greater bondage and damnation. Great struggle awaits all married couples. Good things are equally devil's targets.

At times, problems emerge as soon as a couple gets married. Other times, it comes at the middle of their marriage. Some other times, it may come at the tail end of their marriage. Whichever time, we are encouraged to wrestle and fight war against the devil and not to surrender to him.

For we wrestle not against flesh and blood, but
against principalities, against powers, against
the rulers of the darkness of this world, against
spiritual wickedness in high places

— EPHESIANS 6:12

Fight the good fight of faith, lay hold on eternal
life, whereunto thou art also called, and hast
professed a good profession before many
witnesses

— 1 TIMOTHY 6:12

And why stand we in jeopardy every hour? I
protest by your rejoicing, which I have in Christ
Jesus our Lord, I die daily. If after the manner of
men I have fought with beasts at Ephesus, what
advantageth it me, if the dead rise not? Let us
eat and drink; for tomorrow we die

— 1 CORINTHIANS 15: 30-32

As Christian families, we must depend on God and use right
weapons to fight the devil. Christians who do not expect or
realize how strong the enemy is would likely fail on the day of
battle. God's power to win has been made available to all God's
children and they did not use it.

Blessed be the God and Father of our Lord
Jesus Christ, which according to his abundant
mercy hath begotten us again unto a lively hope

by the resurrection of Jesus Christ from the dead, To an inheritance incorruptible, and undefiled, and that fadeth not away, reserved in heaven for you, Who are kept by the power of God through faith unto salvation ready to be revealed in the last time. Wherein ye greatly rejoice, though now for a season, if need be, ye are in heaviness through manifold temptations: That the trial of your faith, being much more precious than of gold that perisheth, though it be tried with fire, might be found unto praise and honor and glory at the appearing of Jesus Christ: Whom having not seen, ye love; in whom, though now ye see him not, yet believing, ye rejoice with joy unspeakable and full of glory: Receiving the end of your faith, even the salvation of your souls

— 1 PETER 1:3-9

Wherefore the rather, brethren, give diligence to make your calling and election sure: for if ye do these things, ye shall never fall: For so an entrance shall be ministered unto you abundantly into the everlasting kingdom of our Lord and Savior Jesus Christ

— 2 PETER 1:10-11

> Submit yourselves therefore to God. Resist the
> devil, and he will flee from you

— JAMES 4:7

When you discover God's will for your marriage, insist on its manifestation. You must reject other things that oppose God's purpose for your marriage. You have the divine power, authority to confront any power that would seek to redraw the map of your marriage. You must resist things that are against godliness and the promises of God concerning your marriage.

Problems and temptations in marriage should bring you and your wife together in order to help you to know God and prove Him the more. Bearing fruits of the spirit, which is God's nature, makes you more fruitful than barren. Lack of it brings blindness and leads people astray. You must resist the devil and chase him out of your marriage.

F O U R

MARITAL CHALLENGES YOU MUST CONFRONT

I t is not possible to mention all family problems in this book. However, the most important thing is for you to know, define and insist on God's plan, purpose and provisions for your marriage.

[18]And the LORD God said, It is not good that the man should be alone; I will make him a help meet for him. [22]And the rib, which the LORD God had taken from man, made he a woman, and brought her unto the man. [24]Therefore shall a man leave his father and his mother, and shall cleave unto his wife: and they shall be one flesh

— GENESIS 2:18, 22, 24

And he answered and said unto them, Have ye
not read, that he which made them at the
beginning made them male and female, And
said, For this cause shall a man leave father and
mother, and shall cleave to his wife: and they
twain shall be one flesh?

— MATTHEW 19:4-5

For this cause shall a man leave his father and
mother, and shall be joined unto his wife, and
they two shall be one flesh

— EPHESIANS 5:31

When you know God's plan, purpose and provision for your
marriage, you would be able to discern when devil is
establishing his own plan. You should know that no matter the
gravity of problem, conflict or hostility in your marriage,
divorce and separation is not God's perfect will for you. God
who instituted your marriage has already planned and
adequately provided for solutions to all marital problems even
before they rise.

Whatever your family needs is available until you to claim them. You only need to approach problems the right way. The Lord commanded that you leave and cleave to your partner. Therefore, whatever that opposes your obedience to that Word is an enemy. You must resist that power now. Obedience to God's Word brings joy, happiness and peace.

So ought men to love their wives as their own bodies. He that loveth his wife loveth himself. For no man ever yet hated his own flesh; but nourisheth and cherisheth it, even as the Lord the church: For we are members of his body, of his flesh, and of his bones. For this cause shall a man leave his father and mother, and shall be joined unto his wife, and they two shall be one flesh

— EPHESIANS 5:28-31

But from the beginning of the creation God made them male and female. For this cause shall a man leave his father and mother, and cleave to his wife; And they twain shall be one flesh: so then they are no more twain, but one

flesh. What therefore God hath joined together,
let not man put asunder

— MARK 10:6-9

Whoever or whatever that comes between you and your legally married partner is an enemy. Obey the Word of God first. Failure to leave and cleave has caused so many problems in families. It is still a problem in many families today. The problem is that most Christians give devil a place in their marriages when God commanded us not to do so:

Neither give place to the devil

— EPHESIANS 4:27)

Casting all your care upon him; for he careth for you. Be sober, be vigilant; because your adversary the devil, as a roaring lion, walketh about, seeking whom he may devour: Whom resist steadfast in the faith, knowing that the same afflictions are accomplished in your brethren that are in the world

— 1 PETER 5:7-9

Giving the devil a place is a massive problem in many Christian families today. There are husbands and wives who stop greeting themselves because of minor issues. What a pity!

> Greet ye one another with a kiss of charity.
> Peace be with you all that are in Christ Jesus.
> Amen
>
> — 1 PETER 5:14

> Salute one another with a holy kiss. The
> churches of Christ salute you
>
> — ROMANS 16:16

No matter what your partner causes you or how many indignities your partner brings, you must endeavor to great your partner. Kiss one another with a kiss of love. Husbands and wives must salute themselves with a holy kiss. You give devil a huge place in your marriage when you fail to do so. In fact, it is a dangerous thing to do. You must prefer one another; bear each other's burden so that you do not give the devil a place.

Be kindly affectioned one to another with
brotherly love; in honor preferring one another

— ROMANS 12:10

Bear ye one another's burdens, and so fulfill the
law of Christ

— GALATIANS 6:2

You must have a kind affection and prefer one another. Do not wait for your partner to do it first. Let it be a family competition. Always try to do good first. Bearing one another's burden is fulfilling the law of Christ and it comes with blessings. If you do not practice these things, you allow the devil to take down your family through gossips, suspicion, false prophecy and other things. When you give devil a place in the family, he can bring your marriage to a halt. As the Scripture puts it:

For where two or three are gathered together
in my name, there am I in the midst of
them. Then came Peter to him, and said, Lord,
how oft shall my brother sin against me, and I
forgive him? Till seven times? Jesus saith unto
him, I say not unto thee, Until seven times: but,

Until seventy times seven. Therefore is the kingdom of heaven likened unto a certain king, which would take account of his servants. And when he had begun to reckon, one was brought unto him, which owed him ten thousand talents. But forasmuch as he had not to pay, his lord commanded him to be sold, and his wife, and children, and all that he had, and payment to be made. The servant therefore fell down, and worshipped him, saying, Lord, have patience with me, and I will pay thee all. Then the lord of that servant was moved with compassion, and loosed him, and forgave him the debt. But the same servant went out, and found one of his fellow servants, which owed him an hundred pence: and he laid hands on him, and took him by the throat, saying, Pay me that thou owest. And his fellow servant fell down at his feet, and besought him, saying, Have patience with me, and I will pay thee all. And he would not: but went and cast him into prison, until he should pay the debt. So when his fellow servants saw what was done, they were very sorry, and came and told unto their lord all that was done. Then his lord, after that he had called him, said unto him, O thou wicked servant, I forgave thee all

that debt, because thou desiredst me:
Shouldest not thou also have had compassion
on thy fellow servant, even as I had pity on
thee? And his lord was wroth, and delivered him
to the tormentors, until he should pay all that
was due unto him. So likewise shall my heavenly
Father do also unto you, if ye from your hearts
forgive not everyone his brother their
trespasses

— MATTHEW 18:20-35

It is possible that your partner would definitely offend you no matter how holy your partner may be. Nevertheless, God commanded us to forgive one another and continue in love for each other. Even when your partner backslides, becomes careless and offends you, forgive. In order to live in peace and remain a child of God, you must forgive and forget.

This is my commandment, That ye love one
another, as I have loved you. Greater love hath
no man than this that a man lay down his life for
his friends. Ye are my friends, if ye do
whatsoever I command you

— JOHN 15:12-14

Lack of forgiveness brings barriers between husbands and wives. Once any barrier exists, devil occupies every available space and kills the affection between the two of you. At that point, carnal lusts for outsiders would begin to develop. Different problems would start to bud because of a little space. Here, the Scripture revealed the works of the flesh:

> Now the works of the flesh are manifest, which are these; Adultery, fornication, uncleanness, lasciviousness, Idolatry, witchcraft, hatred, variance, emulations, wrath, strife, seditions, heresies, Envyings, murders, drunkenness, revellings, and such like: of the which I tell you before, as I have also told you in time past, that they which do such things shall not inherit the kingdom of God
>
> — GALATIANS 5:19-21

Manifestation of impatience, strife, malice, nagging, bitterness and fighting becomes the norm. The next thing may be pride and failure to pray together. The real agreement in the marriage covenant is affected at this point.

> Verily I say unto you, Whatsoever ye shall bind
> on earth shall be bound in heaven: and
> whatsoever ye shall loose on earth shall be
> loosed in heaven. Again I say unto you, That if
> two of you shall agree on earth as touching
> anything that they shall ask, it shall be done for
> them of my Father which is in heaven
>
> — MATTHEW 18:18-19

At this time, couples start looking for solace outside their marriages. The real purpose for marriage is affected. Strange men, women, house helps and evil people get opportunities to take control over the management of the family. The devil and his evil agents get the opportunity to cause more damage.

In similar cases, a man begins keeping late at nights. The devil destroys family fellowship and provides an evil alternative with himself and his agents. He removes divine marriage comfort and replaces it with demonic comfort. The fulfillment of true living, which is the original plan of God, ceases to exist.

> For the husband is the head of the wife, even as
> Christ is the head of the church: and he is the
> savior of the body. For no man ever yet hated

his own flesh; but nourisheth and cherisheth it,
even as the Lord the church: For we are
members of his body, of his flesh, and of his
bones. For this cause shall a man leave his
father and mother, and shall be joined unto his
wife, and they two shall be one flesh

— EPHESIANS 5:23, 29-31

Two are better than one; because they have a
good reward for their labor. For if they fall, the
one will lift up his fellow: but woe to him that is
alone when he falleth; for he hath not another to
help him up. Again, if two lie together, then they
have heat: but how can one be warm alone?

— ECCLESIASTES 4:9-11

The devil would seek to remove the marriage companionship
and partnership. If they have children, the children would begin
to suffer. Some of them begin to misbehave and become
wayward, rebellious and belligerent. The devil would harvest
their destinies. Sickness, diseases, poverty, suffering and
premature death to life and properties begin to manifest. To
worsen the matter, such couple may end up in separation,
divorce or polygamy.

And Laban gave to Rachel his daughter Bilhah his handmaid to be her maid. And he went in also unto Rachel, and he loved also Rachel more than Leah, and served with him yet seven other years. And when the LORD saw that Leah was hated, he opened her womb: but Rachel was barren. And Leah conceived, and bare a son, and she called his name Reuben: for she said, Surely the LORD hath looked upon my affliction; now therefore my husband will love me

— GENESIS 29:29-32

And when Rachel saw that she bare Jacob no children, Rachel envied her sister; and said unto Jacob, Give me children, or else I die. And Jacob's anger was kindled against Rachel: and he said, Am I in God's stead, who hath withheld from thee the fruit of the womb?

— GENESIS 30:1-2

Polygamy has destroyed so many families and sent them to early graves and hell fire.

FIVE

SOLUTIONS FOR MARITAL CHALLENGES

Consider these few solutions, as you trust God to help you overcome challenges in your marriage. Understand that everyone has a cross to bear in the family. However, if you carry your cross to the Calvary, to Jesus, He will make all things light. Nevertheless, when you drop your cross at Satan's feet in your search for cheap solutions, you will carry a worse cross through eternity.

Jesus said, "Come unto me, all ye that labor and are heavy laden, and I will give you rest. Take my yoke upon you, and learn of me; for I am meek and lowly in heart: and ye shall find rest unto

your souls. For my yoke is easy, and my burden
is light

— MATTHEW 11: 28-30

Do not allow the devil to be your guide. No matter what the problem is, we must comfort, exhort and admonish one another.

Wherefore comfort one another with these
words

— 1 THESSALONIANS 4:18

But exhort one another daily, while it is called
Today; lest any of you be hardened through the
deceitfulness of sin

— HEBREWS 3:13

Not forsaking the assembling of ourselves
together, as the manner of some is; but
exhorting one another: and so much the more,
as ye see the day approaching

— HEBREWS 10:25

> And I myself also am persuaded of you, my brethren, that ye also are full of goodness, filled with all knowledge, able also to admonish one another

— ROMANS 15:14

> Let the word of Christ dwell in you richly in all wisdom; teaching and admonishing one another in psalms and hymns and spiritual songs, singing with grace in your hearts to the Lord

— COLOSSIANS 3:16

Our comfort comes from God and that provides our comfort for each other. You must learn to reject any other comfort or comforter that is not from God. Comfort one another based on the Word of God. Do not forsake the Assembly of God's children because of problems. Do not take anyone to consult any other power except the power of God. Do not accept any solution that is not of God. Always insist on God's way with God's people.

In your trials, fill your thought with the goodness and your knowledge of God, and refuse to be discouraged. Fill your thoughts with the Word of God. When you succeed in preserving your marriage without compromise, you would fulfill the purpose of marriage and make it to heaven. Perhaps, your marriage is messed up already. You can still make amends. Jesus is never too late or too early. Delay is not denial.

> And when he came to himself, he said, How many hired servants of my father's have bread enough and to spare, and I perish with hunger! I will arise and go to my father, and will say unto him, Father, I have sinned against heaven, and before thee, And am no more worthy to be called thy son: make me as one of thy hired servants. And he arose, and came to his father. But when he was yet a great way off, his father saw him, and had compassion, and ran, and fell on his neck, and kissed him
>
> — LUKE 15:17-20

God is ready to accept you back. God expects you to make your ways right before Him and come out of sin. The consistent teaching of God's Word is that marriage is a lifetime contract.

If you preserve your marriage, despite all odds, the Lord will answer your prayers and make you happy to enjoy your marriage in an old age.

PRAYERS TO PRESERVE YOUR MARRIAGE

Bible references: <u>Exodus 23:25-26</u>; <u>Deuteronomy 28:1-14</u>

Begin with praise and worship

End every step with prayers as you led

STEP 1

I break and loose my partner and me from every unprofitable association, in the name of Jesus. I disgrace the power of darkness that has vowed to scatter my marriage, in the name of Jesus. Every demonic authority that is working against my marriage, be frustrated, in the name of Jesus. I terminate evil control over my marriage, in the name of Jesus. Let the bewitchment and manipulation of my marriage expire, in the name of Jesus. Fire of God, burn every enemy of my marriage, in the name of Jesus. Any evil relationship designed to break my marriage, break, in the name of Jesus. Let strangers in my marriage be disgraced, in the name of Jesus. Any evil soul-tie that is attacking my marriage, break by force, in the name of Jesus. I terminate ungodly relationships that are creating problems in my marriage, in the name of Jesus. Any evil society that is causing trouble in my marriage, be frustrated, in the name of Jesus. I expose and disgrace hidden problems that are attacking my marriage, in the name of Jesus. Any evil counsel that is affecting my marriage, I reject you, in the name of Jesus. I break and loose my marriage from undue interference of our parents, in the name of Jesus. Any demonic in-law that has vowed to destroy my marriage, be destroyed, in the name of Jesus. Let every curse that is placed upon my marriage expire immediately, in the name of Jesus. I cast out forever demons that are attacking my marriage, in the name of Jesus. I disengage my marriage from any marriage in the spiritual realm, in the name of Jesus.

STEP 2

Let every covenant and curse that is attacking my marriage be broken, in the name of Jesus. I command my partner to be delivered from bewitchments and evil traps, in the name of Jesus. Let every fake love that exists in my marriage expire and die, in the name of Jesus. Every evil yoke that is placed upon my marriage, break to pieces, in the name of Jesus. Let the fire of God burn every evil spirit that is fighting my marriage, in the name of Jesus. I cast out every spirit of misunderstanding in my marriage, in the name of Jesus. Let every demon that has followed me since my wedding day die, in the name of Jesus. I receive deliverance from the mistakes I have ever made in this marriage, in the name of Jesus. Blood of Jesus, flow into my foundation and deliver my marriage, in the name of Jesus. Any strongman that is militating against my marriage, die, in the name of Jesus. Any evil arrow that was fired at my marriage, backfire, in the name of Jesus. Every sin that has followed us into our marriage, receive pardon, in the name of Jesus. Let the spirit of anger, pride, domineering character and other works of the flesh cease in my marriage, in the name of Jesus. Any evil utterance ever spoken against my marriage, expire, in the name of Jesus.

STEP 3

I silence evil voices that are tormenting my marriage, in the name of Jesus. Lord Jesus, arise and take over my marriage forever, in the name of Jesus. O Lord, help me to keep the vows of my marriage, in the name of Jesus. I disgrace agents of separation and divorce in my marriage, in the name of Jesus. Let every problem that is attacking my marriage die, in the name of Jesus. Blood of Jesus, speak everlasting peace into my marriage, in the name of Jesus.

THANK YOU!

I'd like to use this time to thank you for purchasing my books and helping my ministry and work. Any copy of my book you buy helps to fund my ministry and family, as well as offering much-needed inspiration to keep writing. My family and I are very thankful, and we take your assistance very seriously.

You have already accomplished so much, but I would appreciate an honest review of some of my books through the link below. This is critical since reviews reflect how much an author's work is respected.

Please visit https://www.amazon.com/review/create-review?asin=B09TDW5K5Z or CLICK HERE TO LEAVE A REVIEW

Please be aware that I read and value all comments and reviews. You can always post a review even though you haven't finished the book yet, and then edit your reviews later.

Once again, here is the link:

Please visit https://www.amazon.com/review/create-review?asin=B09TDW5K5Z or CLICK HERE TO LEAVE A REVIEW

Thank you so much as you spare a precious moment of your time and may God bless you and meet you at the very point of your need.

You can also send me an email to prayermadu@yahoo.com if you encounter any difficulty while writing your review.

OTHER BOOKS BY PRAYER MADUEKE

1. 100 Days Prayers to Wake Up Your Lazarus
2. 15 Deliverance Steps to Everlasting Life
3. 21/40 Nights of Decrees and Your Enemies Will Surrender
4. 35 Deliverance Steps to Everlasting Rest
5. 35 Special Dangerous Decrees
6. 40 Prayer Giants
7. Alone with God
8. Americans, May I Have Your Attention Please
9. Avoid Academic Defeats
10. Because You Are Living Abroad
11. Biafra of My Dream
12. Breaking Evil Yokes
13. Call to Renew Covenant
14. Command the Morning, Day and Night
15. Community Liberation and Solemn Assembly
16. Comprehensive Deliverance
17. Confront and Conquer Your Enemy
18. Contemporary Politicians' Prayers for Nation Building
19. Crossing the Hurdles
20. Dangerous Decrees to Destroy Your Destroyers (Series)
21. Dealing with Institutional Altars
22. Deliverance by Alpha and Omega

FREE EBOOKS

In order to say a 'Thank You' for purchasing *Prayers to Preserve your Marriage,* I offer these books to you in appreciation.

> **Click here or go to madueke.com/free-gift to download the eBooks now** <

CHRISTIAN COUNSELLING

We were created for a greater purpose than only survival and God wants us to live a full life.

If you need prayer or counselling, or if you have any other inquiries, please visit the counselling page on my website madueke.com/counselling to know when I will be available for a phone call.

EMAIL NEWSLETTER & ANNOUNCEMENTS

Never miss a message from me again! People who read my newsletters say that they have been one of the most important tools in their Christian walk. The best part is that a subscription is, and always will be, completely free. As a subscriber on my mailing list, you'll be the first to hear about my new book releases, be invited to my weekly prayer sessions, and get reminders about my blog posts and other helpful information.

To subscribe, please visit the newsletter page on my website madueke.com/newsletter.

AN INVITATION TO BECOME A MINISTRY PARTNER

In response to several calls from readers of my books on how to collaborate with this ministry, we are grateful to provide our ministry's bank details.

Be assured that our continued prayers for you will be answered according to God's Word, and as you remain faithful by sowing seeds of faith, God will never forget your labors of love in Christ Jesus.

Send your Seeds to:

In Nigeria & Africa

Bank Name: **Access Bank**

Account Name: **Prayer Emancipation Missions**

Account Number: **0692638220**

In the United States & the rest of the World

Bank Name: **Bank of America**

Account Name: **Roseline C. Madueke**

Account Number: **483079070578**

You can also visit the donation page on my website to donate online: www.madueke.com/donate.